For Marge McCarthy—D.D.M.

To my late grandmother—C.G.

Text © 2005 Dandi Daley Mackall.

Illustrations © 2005 Claudine Gévry.

© 2005 Standard Publishing, Cincinnati, Ohio.

A division of Standex International Corporation.

All rights reserved. Printed in China.

Project editor: Robin Stanley.

Cover and interior design: Marissa Bowers.

Scripture quotations are taken from The Holy Bible, New Living Translation, copyright © 1996.

Used by permission of Tyndale House Publishers, Inc., Wheaton, IL. 60189.

All rights reserved.

12 11 10 09 08 07 06 05   9 8 7 6 5 4 3 2 1

ISBN 0-7847-1654-4

Library of Congress Cataloging-in-Publication Data on file.

I can talk to God by
PRAYING JESUS' WAY

Written by
Dandi Daley Mackall

Pictures by
Claudine Gévry

Standard
PUBLISHING
Bringing The Word to Life™

Cincinnati, Ohio

Lord, I'm not sure how to pray;
I want to do it right.
Fold my hands? Or kneel like this?
Or wish with all my might?

I guess I'm not the only one
to wonder what to say.
Even Jesus' closest friends asked,

"Teach us how to pray."

So Jesus taught a special prayer
that kind of goes this way . . .

Once when Jesus had been out praying, one of his disciples...said, "Lord, teach us to pray."

Luke 11:1

God's way up in heaven and so far away!
But since he's my Father,
it's easy to pray.

And we talk in the day.

My Father in heaven,
I'll pray.

Our Father in heaven...

Matthew 6:9

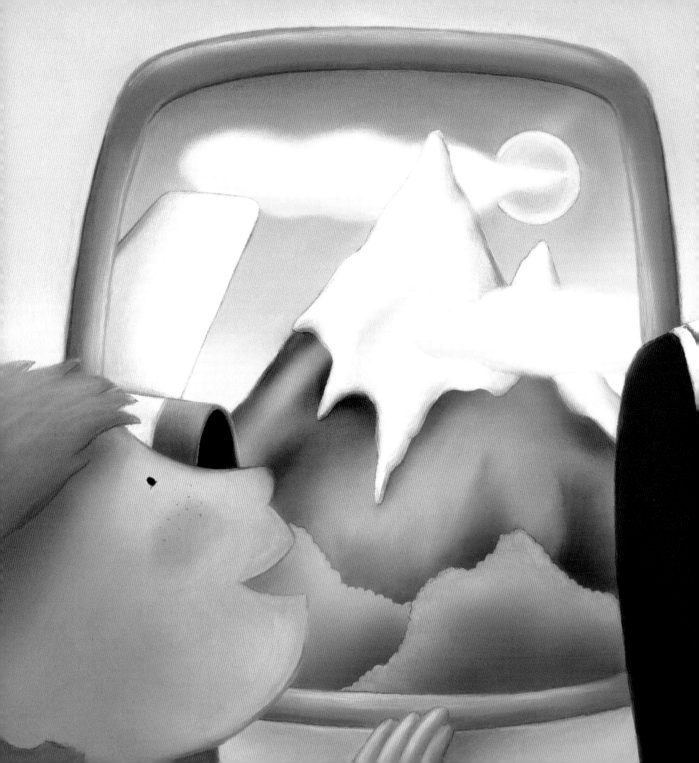

God's super important, and so when I call,
I'll think of his oceans and mountains so tall.
The world is amazing, and he made it all!

I'll honor your name
when I pray.

May your name be honored.

Matthew 6:9

I like it on earth, but I'm eager to see
the wonders of heaven just waiting for me!
I'll give God a hug, and I'll sit on his knee.

I'll pray that your
kingdom comes soon.

May your Kingdom come soon.

Matthew 6:10

What goes on in heaven
should happen down here.
I'll talk about Jesus without any fear . . .

And give God my praise with a rollicking cheer!

May earth be a lot
more like heaven.

May your will be done here on earth, just as it is in heaven.

Matthew 6:10

God makes all the food that I'll need for today.
I'll bow down my head to give thanks as I pray.
And as for tomorrow, that's too far away!

Please give me my
food for today.

Give us our food for today.

Matthew 6:11

I know that I'm weak, but my Jesus is strong.
I'll tell God I'm sorry for things I do wrong.
And when he forgives me, my heart sings a song!

Father, forgive me,
I'll pray.

And forgive us our sins...

Matthew 6:12

So I'll forgive others, 'cause that's only fair.
With all God's forgiveness, there's plenty to share.
If somebody hurts me, I'll pull out this prayer.

I'll pray, Father,
help me forgive.

God helps me want more than
to have my own way.

He helps me say no to what isn't okay.
He whispers my name and reminds me to pray.

Please keep me
from sinning, I'll say.

And don't let us yield to temptation.

Matthew 6:13

I know God protects me. He's watching me, too,
and helping to make me more loving and true.
He's showing me daily what Jesus would do!

God, keep me near you,
I'll pray.

But deliver us from the evil one.

Matthew 6:13

For yours is the kingdom,
and yours is the power.

I know God is listening hour after hour.

Yours is the glory,
and yours is the praise.

That's how I'll talk to God all of my days.

Amen.

For yours is the Kingdom and the Power and the glory forever. Amen.

Matthew 6:13

Luke 11:1, 2

Once when Jesus had been out praying, one of his disciples came to him as he finished and said, "Lord, teach us to pray, just as John taught his disciples."

He said,

"This is how you should pray . . ."

Matthew 6:9-13

"Our Father in heaven,

may your name be honored.

May your Kingdom come soon.

May your will be done here on earth,

just as it is in heaven.

Give us our food for today,

and forgive us our sins,

just as we have forgiven those who have sinned against us.

And don't let us yield to temptation,

but deliver us from the evil one.

For yours is the Kingdom and the power and the glory forever. Amen."